# DAVE PELZER'S

*Life Lessons*

Other titles by the same author

# DAVE PELZER'S

## *Life Lessons*

### from a man who knows

Element
An Imprint of HarperCollins*Publishers*
77–85 Fulham Palace Road,
Hammersmith, London W6 8JB

element™

and *Element*
are trademarks of HarperCollins*Publishers* Ltd

Material taken from *Help Yourself*, originally published in
the USA by Dutton, a member of Penguin Putnam Inc.;
published by Thorsons 2001. This revised edition published
by Element 2002

1 3 5 7 9 10 8 6 4 2

A catalogue record of this book is
available from the British Library

ISBN 0-00-714691-4

Printed and bound in Great Britain by
Martins The Printers Ltd, Berwick upon Tweed

This book is dedicated to my lovely wife, Marsha, and my incredible son, Stephen, who both guide and inspire me in ways that only God knows.

This book is also dedicated to you, the reader, in the sincere hope that you, too, can live a more fulfilling, productive life that you truly deserve.

# Foreword

This book is simple and straightforward. There is no New Age psychobabble; just me speaking directly to you. This book contains the best of the lessons I have learnt, and I offer them to you as a source of daily inspiration.

Each of the small sections within this book represents a different life lesson. I hope that by passing on the knowledge I have gained from my experiences, I can inspire you to take charge of your life. My message is simple: first, get rid of the garbage in your life; next, discover what

you want out of your life; and, finally, celebrate who you are and what you have.

As simple as this book may be, its deeper purpose is addressing your attitude and changing the way you look at life. While I pray that this book will help you through life's challenges, I know it will not solve every problem that suddenly arises. (I wish it could.) For life is ever changing.

At the end of the day, only you can make the changes that lead to fulfilment. Outside influences can only take you so far. The drive has to come from within you.

I hope this little book can offer you support in the bad times and the courage to withstand whatever life throws at you. Happiness can be yours; in the final analysis, it's up to you.

# Introduction

## Be Resilient

I know something about resilience. For the first twelve years of my life I was subjected to practically every form of continuous physical and psychological torture you could imagine. I should have died. After I was rescued from my alcoholic mother and was fortunate enough to be placed in the care of others, there were a few who boasted that because of my extreme situation I would end up either dead or in prison – the odds against me were insurmountable.

I never saw it that way.

If I learned anything from my unfortunate childhood it is that there is nothing that can dominate or conquer the human spirit. How can you expect to be a good parent, an astute businessperson, or achieve your greatness if you do not focus and harness your inner potential? This is the essence of the message I wish to present to you.

Ever since I was a boy, living at times minute by minute, from the depths of my soul I believed that if I were to live, if I could overcome all that I had suffered, then anything else had to be better. In other words, I learned the value of personal responsibility, resilience and gratitude. Only I had to learn at a younger age than most.

## Learn to Fly!

As a child, because I lived in a garage and never played sports, I had limited co-ordination. When I was placed in foster care, because of my lack of developmental skills I could not play a simple game of catch, let alone toss a football. Yet years later as a young adult, after a great deal of self-determination, I was fortunate enough to serve my country as an elite aircrew member, entrusted to fly highly classified missions for the United States Air Force. Days after I turned eighteen, I discovered my childhood case had been identified as one of the most severe instances of child abuse in the state of California. And nearly twenty years from the day I was rescued, I was privileged enough to be selected as one of the Ten Outstanding Young Americans, for my efforts involving child-abuse awareness and prevention.

I am not revealing my former experiences to extract sympathy or mentioning my accomplishments for the purpose of feeding my ego. My lovely wife, teenage son and my higher power keep me grounded. I only offer these examples because, if you are going to spend your precious time and hard-earned money on this book, you should at least be given the decency to know your author's qualifications.

# No One Is Perfect

Even with all that I've experienced, I still have much to learn. Just like you, I am not perfect. I have problems that I have to address on a daily basis – my self-esteem, being a good husband and father, issues pertaining to my health and my demanding business – which at times can be overwhelming. I simply try to deal with things as best I can.

I am not special in any way. I do not possess some magic crystal that contains the secrets of the cosmos. The truth be told: no one has all the answers. There is no such thing as a perfect life. I am simply a regular person who wants to relate to you what I have learned and how you may apply my experiences and life lessons in your professional and private life. I hope that this little book will help you through the bumps of life, showing you that you have the capability to better yourself no matter what the odds.

# Let Go of Your Past

Every one of us has a past. All of us have had our share of problems. Loved ones pass away. Parents divorce. Others who don't strive as hard and don't deserve the prized promotion receive it. You name it, all of us has endured the deepest of pain. But are you a prisoner to your past or stronger and wiser because of it?

The single most critical element I have found that prevents individuals from achieving their greatness is unresolved issues.

It doesn't matter who you are, you can never reach your full potential unless you deal with and rid yourself of whatever may be troubling you. You cannot move forward until you free yourself from the shackles of your past.

*Let go of a
past you cannot
change.*

# Deal with Everyday Problems

All of us tend to suppress problems rather than deal with them as soon as they unexpectedly 'pop up'. Every one of us at one time or another has found ourselves in uncomfortable situations that we did not deal with – problems stemming from work or personal matters that, because we haven't dealt with them, become so overwhelming that we end up so consumed by the situation, to the point that it affects our attitude and every aspect of our day.

I believe if we learn to deal with the everyday problems of life, it helps us all the more when something more arduous comes along.

Settle your problems
as promptly and as
thoroughly as you
are able.

# Rest Your Mind

Why is it that when you have a problem you can't get your mind to let go? The basic answer is your brain is simply trying to find the precise solution to that particular problem. If the problem is overwhelming, your mind will not function to its full capacity because it is being drawn to the dilemma it is focused on.

With all that every one of us does in a single day, with all the problems that bombard us, if we do not learn to rest our mind, we will run ourselves into the ground.

This is why I cannot stress enough the value of a good night's sleep. With a recharged battery you are all the better when it comes to tackling whatever comes your way.

In the midst of
fighting life's battles,
relax.

# Alleviate the Stress of Your Day

You will never be able to solve all your problems to your liking. And at times you will feel overwhelmed and frustrated. That's life. So what can you do to alleviate some of that pressure? Two words: *controlled eruptions*.

Opening up not only helps you relieve that pent-up anxiety, but sometimes it can be just enough to get you through.

Every day try to do something that will alleviate the stress of your day. Screech at that radio talk-show host, work out at the gym, take a stroll anywhere you feel at peace. Within reason, alleviate some of that pressure to clear your mind and enable it to focus on the events of your day.

---

Vent your frustrations
in a controlled yet
cleansing manner.

---

## 'I Feel Much Better!'

My wife, Marsha: she shops. She has a weakness for makeup, shoes and anything within the confines of a mall. But at least Marsha comes home happier than when she left, and proudly proclaims her mantra 'I feel much better!'

On a more serious note, by leaving the office Marsha gets away from her pressure-filled environment. In her car Marsha applies that time to decompress as she sings out loud. In a psychological sense, walking the length of the mall several times at a brisk pace helps Marsha diminish her stress all the more.

# Cleanse Your Soul

When I listen to folks who tell me their predicaments, I try to get them to open up, to tell me everything, rather than scratch the surface. For the most part, when we get to the core of the issue, we realize the situation that we held on to for so long, that caused us so much pain, is not as bad as it seems or seemed at the time.

For lack of a better word, it's what I call *purging*. It is imperative you *psychologically purge* yourself of whatever is ailing you.

If you have situations that seem to pull you down or if you seem tied to something in your past, if you do not open up and purge yourself from the recesses of your soul, you are most likely to be a slave of your experience.

Have the courage to
purify yourself of
whatever may be
holding you back.

# We All Have a Choice

All of us have had unpleasant experiences and situations that we have had to deal with on a daily basis. And many of us have been subjected to a negative environment, such as an unhappy childhood or growing up in a very poor environment. But even with the best of surroundings, it is the individual who decides his or her own fate.

When it comes to dealing with negative surroundings, I believe it boils down to three options: we become a product of a negative environment; we find a way out of the environment, or adjust to it the best we can.

While adverse surroundings play an important role in our lives, if we are willing we do not have to be dominated by them. In fact, we can use them to make us strive for something better.

If you have been subjected to negative surroundings, use them to make you strive for something better.

## Striving for Something Better

*Being exposed to a negative setting does not mean you are either destined for a life of crime or doomed to an unfulfilled life. United States Secretary of State and former chairman of the Joint Chiefs of Staff General Colin Powell, the first African American to hold such offices, was raised in a rat-infested ghetto in Harlem, New York. His parents – immigrants from Jamaica – did all they could for their son, yet it was Colin who had to decide his fate. Some may say it would have been understandable for young Colin to have been swallowed up by the gritty streets of New York or fallen through the cracks of society, but he, wanting something more for himself, enlisted in the army, immersed himself in college, and eventually came up through the ranks to lead America's armed forces in operations Desert Shield and Desert Storm.*

# Maintain Your Distance from Negative Settings

Some people who can't seem to let go of their negative past may find them-selves doomed because of it. Unless we have the knowledge, courage and constant discipline to maintain our distance from negative settings, there is a chance – not an excuse – that we can become a carbon copy of that environment.

When it comes to breaking away from a negative environment, sometimes we have to do just that, and as hard and as emotional as it may be, we have to make a clean break.

_Limit your exposure to negative settings and, if necessary, make a clean break._

# Overcome Your Guilt

All of us have regrets and I'm sure we have said or done things we are not proud of. If you find yourself unable to move forward or feel 'pulled in' because of your past environment, ask yourself: *Was there anything I could have done to prevent the situation?* If the answer is yes, then do something different now and become a better person because of it. If your response is no, then you have your answer. Next, ask yourself: *Did I do the best I could at the time?* If the answer is yes, then let the past

go. If the response is no, again, learn something from it and *do* something positive about
the situation the next time.

If you feel guilty about what has transpired, make amends as best you can, and if possible turn it around and use it as a stepping stone to make things better.

# 'Why Was I Spared?'

*A few years ago I had the honour of meeting a woman named Michelle, who is a survivor of the Holocaust. When she was a child, toward the end of World War II in Europe, the Nazis put Michelle and her mother on a train that was to be sent to a death camp. Michelle's mother gave her life to save her young daughter Michelle. When I had the opportunity to speak with Michelle, she revealed a crushing force that had weighed upon her all of her life. 'Why was I spared when so many others died?' After she poured out her feelings, I held her and asked her the question 'Was there anything you could have done to prevent what had happened?'* Michelle shook her head no. *'Then you can do no more.'*

# Stop Being a Please-aholic!

Making sure you don't become a prisoner to a negative environment also means being careful that you don't become a 'please-aholic'. So many folks, myself included, who are or were exposed to a negative setting, with or without knowing may find themselves overcompensating by trying to obtain other people's approval – especially those who make them feel inferior.

It's important for all of us to apply ourselves, with everything we have, every day, but we need to channel our efforts for the right cause. And while it's vital for all of us to be kind and display manners while being humble, we should do so *without* giving ourselves away in the process. The truth is, no matter what you do for the sole purpose of having others admire you, your efforts will most likely be in vain.

*Don't give yourself
away in the vain hope
of appeasing others.*

# Be Your Own Person

There can be endless reasons why folks may not like us, no matter what we do. In the end, we must have the will to simply be ourselves.

When you please others in the hope of being accepted, you lose your self-worth in the process. As elementary as this sounds: to help yourself, you have to be yourself. Be the best person you can possibly be. Stand up for yourself. Without being rude and arrogant, speak your piece. Every day do your best and if there are those who disagree with you, it's not the end of the world.

By being more self-assured, you're not only taking a stand but you will actually learn more quickly to adapt to a negative environment.

Make and maintain
the commitment of
being your own person.

# Never Go to Bed Upset

When we are in heated disagreements with
the ones we love or the ones close to us – our
significant others, our children, parents,
those at work, our best friends – it is important to try to resolve our issues as soon
as possible, before the situation comes to a
head; before it leads to anger, outrage and
feelings of hatred.

Try your best not to allow the sun to set
without trying to find some form of resolution
to your issues. You may not be able to solve

all the problems, but by addressing the situation, rather than burying it, you can prevent feelings of animosity taking root.

Constantly do your best to resolve whatever problems you have.

## Compromise

Rather than hold a grudge and waste your time hashing over who did what to whom, get to the core of the frustration. If necessary, be the bigger person – compromise and give a little. Don't shut that person down. Don't let the powerful negative emotions get the best of you. Open your heart and make an effort to resolve the situation as best as you can.

When dealing with those close to me, I have learned that sometimes the smallest things –

a touch, hug or a kind word – can make a world of difference. Resolve the matter before it envelopes you. Before your feelings become ensconced ... and perhaps lead to hate.

Compromise, at least
just enough to make
things better.

# Hate No One!

Of all the life lessons I have been fortunate enough to learn, the single most powerful, most important one is: hate no one!

I believe hate is like cancer: it can spread and kill a person, one 'life cell', one day, at a time. If hatred goes unchecked it can take over one's life. If you hate today, it's easier for you to hate tomorrow, then the next day and the next, until you've wasted your entire life by becoming dominated by what you detested in the first place. How can you live a productive life and all that goes with it, if you are controlled by such intense feelings as hate? Personally, I don't call that much of a life.

Hate, just like cancer,
if not dealt with early
on, kills one day at
a time.

# Letting Go of Hate

I recently read an article in a national magazine that addressed the issue of letting go of hate. The article made reference to Mitchell Wright, the widower of Shannon Wright, a teacher who was killed at the school shooting in Jonesboro, Arkansas. Before Shannon died she said to Mitchell, 'Take care of Zane,' their baby boy. While there may be some who would probably say Mitchell has every reason to hate those who have caused such great pain and loss in his life and his son's life, it is Mitchell who said, 'If you let hate and anger build in you, that's a very strong sin. I need to be able to totally forgive. Well, if I lose that, then I can't take care of Zane.'

# Choose to Forgive

When I stress the importance of *forgiveness*, I do so mainly to encourage freeing yourself. To me, forgiveness does not mean forgetting what may have happened to or against you. But with time, maturity and a different perspective we can free ourselves of emotions that can only lead to great suffering. When we choose to forgive, it frees us to not only live a more fulfilled life, but, more importantly, to rid ourselves of animosity.

Get closure with the person you need to forgive. Pick up that phone, talk to that person, write that letter even if you never mail it. Hug that person. Lower your defences. Listen with your heart and an objective mind. Just do whatever you have to do to expel those bad feelings from your system. Every day, wipe your slate clean.

---

*Forgiveness allows you
to be cleansed and
helps to ease your pain.*

---

# You Do Not Need to Be a Victim

Just because bad things happen to you doesn't mean you are destined to be a victim. Many predicaments in our lives are unexpected and we may not be up to the initial challenge. It may even seem overwhelming. But as individuals we can either run from our situations, bury them, or face our problems and deal with them accordingly.

Maybe it's a good thing that life isn't fair. When you're behind a little, that's when you're focused on what's important. When you're hungry for that one thing, that single element, whatever it is, it's astounding what you can achieve! And when you dedicate yourself to your cause, no matter the outcome, you can be proud that no one, no one on this planet, did what you did. You earned it. Against all odds, you did what you had to do.

Before you quit on yourself when life isn't fair, exhaust all your options for making things happen.

# Resolve to Make Things Happen for You

At the end of the day it is *you* and you alone who have to *do* whatever it takes to accomplish your goal. Not your teacher, your parents, those at work, your spiritual leader, close friends, spouse, guru or psychic advisors. It's you!

Make this sentence your daily axiom, stating it aloud: 'Whatever/whoever can only help me so far, can only do so much for me.'

I believe we need to be more responsible and rely more on ourselves. *In the end those in our lives can only help us so far.*

Yes, it *may* seem impossible or hard to do, but when there is something that you want, that one thing you crave, ask yourself this: *how badly do I want it?* If your desire is that great, if it burns deep inside of you, day in and day out, then *you* will most likely find a way to make it happen.

*If you want it, you have to make it possible.*

## 'I Can Only Help You So Far'

Years ago when my son, Stephen, turned ten, as we were talking about how proud I was of him and how far he had come, I said something that seemed to resonate from within him. 'Stephen', I stated, 'you're ten years old now. You know right from wrong, good from evil, and the repercussions of your actions. I will always help you as best as I can. But realize this: from this moment on, you are a young man. And as a young man, understand that I can only help you so far.'

# Give Yourself the Credit You Deserve

You may not even realize or may have forgotten that you have already accomplished a great deal in your life. Remember, the smallest things can make a world of difference. And a little bit of struggle is not a bad thing. Take a moment. Ask yourself, *what have I accomplished?*

Give yourself the credit you deserve, and instead of contaminating yourself by saying what you can't do, ask yourself *what* can you not accomplish when you truly commit to that one thing?

I have the highest respect for anybody who knows what they want and at least tries, even if it's against all the odds, to better themselves. Win or lose, they take a few hits, they fall down, but they get up from the mat, battered and bruised, they brush themselves off, tap into their inner drive and give it what they've got. *That's* what counts.

When fighting to make your life better, give yourself the credit you deserve.

# Know What You Want

What do *you* want out of life? I am not talking short-term goals or long-range, five-to-ten-year master plans; rather what is that singular thing that you desire? Did you know that you have four to five times better chance of reaching your goals, of achieving financial success, of fulfilling your dreams, for the simple fact that you know what you want and you are determined to make it happen.

I have found over the years the unequivocal 'thing' that folks want out of life is:

TO BE HAPPY! That's it. When we're happy does it truly matter how much we have, what people think of us, or what we look like? When we are happy with who we are and what we have in our life right now, isn't everything else a bonus?

Know what you want
and be determined to
make it happen.

# Invest in Yourself

Sit down, spend some quality time with your-self, and discover from the deepest recesses of your heart *what is truly important to you.* Find it. Hold on to it. Live it. No matter how hard it may be, keep a positive attitude. Don't take setbacks personally. Look at them as opportunities to see what you're truly made of. Never lose sight of your objective. But *please* don't lose yourself in the process – stay grounded and appreciative of the every-day 'little' things in life. Don't be too hard on yourself, for you will fall down; yet it is getting up that truly matters.

Find something, do something, every single day that brings you one step closer to your goal and reward yourself for your valiant efforts, no matter how insignificant they may seem.

Take the time and energy to truly invest in your most important asset: yourself.

# Dedicate Yourself to Your Cause

There is no such thing as an overnight success. The cold truth is if you make it overnight, you can lose it just as fast. If there is one key to success, one key to obtaining your desires, then it's one word. Work. Work, work, work, work, work. In everything you do, apply yourself. Harness your ambitions, be enthusiastic and dedicate yourself to your cause.

But what if your mind-set was to accomplish your objective with seemingly little effort, and it merely became a part of your everyday routine? How do you do something that seems so overwhelming? You do a little here and a little there until your overwhelming, arduous, impossible challenges become your everyday routine. In a nutshell, that's it.

Attempt the so-called 'impossible' until it becomes an everyday part of your life.

## Absolute Devotion

Just a few years ago, immediately after Tiger Woods won the Masters in Augusta, Georgia, everyone bombarded him. I read how one person asked Tiger, 'Son, what's it like to pick up a golf club and start whacking those balls as well as you do?' Tiger smiled and replied, 'Sir, I've been hitting balls for about nineteen years.' 'Nineteen years?!' the older man exclaimed, 'Son, how old are you?' Again smiling, Tiger answers, 'Twenty-one, sir.'

Think about it: when Tiger was a toddler, his father, Earl, would teach him how to hold a *putter, swing a club, address the ball and sink a putt. Every day, Tiger played golf. Tiger devoted his time and efforts to his art. He sacrificed a lot in the process, but paid the price to achieve his greatness.*

# Don't Give Your Best Away

We all have desires. And I believe all of us have the best of intentions. But the reality is that we give our best away. No one takes it from us; we give it away. We allow self-doubt, time, situations or whatever else to erode our dreams. We quit on ourselves. We carry regret, regret turns into frustration, frustration into anger, anger into sorrow. And all the while life has slipped away from us.

We've lost one of life's most precious gifts:
the excitement, the fear, the heart-pounding
sensation of taking a step outside our protective womb. We give up our desire to do
*something* to better ourselves.

And all you have to do is *apply yourself.*

Work, work, work, work. Whether it's your
marriage, interpersonal relationships, raising
kids, your health, schooling or your career,
apply yourself. With all that you are able to
do, apply a little extra, just an extra nudge,
every day, and see the difference it makes
in your attitude and the outcome of your
achievements.

No one takes anything away from us, unless we give up on ourselves first.

# Go the Distance

Life is not now nor ever will be black and white. Just as with an aeroplane, sometimes a crosswind may blow us off course or we hit an unexpected air pocket and lose our altitude. Yet all we have to do is check our direction and make a slight adjustment to get where we want to go.

Every day when you're climbing that ladder of success you will hit some peaks and valleys. Every day you're working, you're studying, you're scrimping, you're saving, paying your dues and *bam*: life just slaps you down on the mat. It's not fair, it's not right, but what are you going to do about it? My advice: brush yourself off, get up, and *go the distance*. Part of the thrill of success is the journey of the struggle. If it were easy everyone would be doing it.

---

When you hit that
unexpected bump in the
road, it's only a bump
in the road.

---

## 'Look How Far You've Come!'

Some folks quit on themselves even though they're so close to achieving their goals. I had a friend, Don, who wanted to get rid of a hundred pounds. After taking control and persisting in his lifelong battle, Don got rid of sixty pounds, but after a run of bad luck at work and some problems at home, he felt like a loser and wanted to throw in the towel.

When Don moaned that getting rid of sixty pounds wasn't that much and complained how far he was from his goal, I gave him a pair of thirty pound dumbbells. 'Here', I said, 'hold these for *a while. Or better yet, tie them around your neck. Heavy, eh?, I smiled. 'Now, THAT'S how far you've come!'*

# Be Happy

Why is it a lot of folks are so unhappy? Why are there great numbers of people who, no matter what they have or whatever they strive to achieve, seem so unfulfilled? I'm guessing unresolved issues would play a major role, but part of the solution could be that maybe the older we get, the more complacent, hopeless and despondent we become. For one reason or another we forget to be happy.

Now, I'm not saying you should walk through life grinning from ear to ear, but I am saying to at least be happy in your quests and the world you live in right now, today. Don't wait to get that job, pass that exam, marry that person, buy that car or survive some immense crisis for you to be appreciative. Because while you think you are truly happy, you are only basing your happiness on your surroundings or the situation and not yourself as a person. And don't you deserve better than that?

---

Be happy with who
you are and what
you have in your life
right now!

---

# Adopt a Positive, Upbeat Attitude

So many of us work hard, provide for our families and sacrifice ourselves to the hilt, so much so that we can easily surrender our inner passions and happiness in the process.

I advise that in all of your efforts as you apply yourself in areas of health, in saving for the future, studying for that test, and so on, each and every day do the same on your positive, upbeat attitude. As always, continue to better yourself but do so *now* by being aware of your emotional state. Replace negative attitudes with positive ones. As you are well aware: as bad as things are, they could be a lot worse. And griping and complaining will not get you out of it, but a simple optimistic attitude can turn things around.

A consistent, positive
attitude makes a world
of difference.

## Spreading a Bit of Cheer

Years ago, before the comedian actress Gilda Radner passed away from her battle with cancer, she formed groups with others who, like her, were fighting the disease, and together they found a sense of happiness and reprieve from their situations. It didn't change the fact that these brave people had to deal with their life-threatening disease every day, but spreading a bit of cheer among themselves made their circumstances the more tolerable. In one interview I heard Ms Radner say, 'I look at it this way: as I'm fighting cancer, I think of all the money I'm *saving on shampoo.' To this day Gilda's disposition has touched countless others who are surviving cancer with dignity and feeling more fulfilled.*

# Live the Best Life That You Can Today

Years ago I read a poem that to this day has had a profound affect on my life. 'If I had my life to live over ... I'd relax, I would limber up ... I would take fewer things seriously ... I would climb more mountains and swim more rivers ... I would eat more ice cream ... I would pick more daisies.' This poem was written by Nadine Stair, an eighty-five-year-old woman whose words encouraged me to see and live life through new eyes.

The primary reason why I'm hammering away at you to be content with who you are and what you have in your life right now is there are no guarantees when you go to sleep at night that you are going to wake up tomorrow morning. None!

Don't allow every little thing to get to you, drag you down and consume your life. There may not be a tomorrow to count on, so live the best life that you can today.

There are no
guarantees for tomorrow,
so appreciate all that
you have and do all
that you can today!

# Think Differently!

Did you know that at least seventy-five percent of our thoughts when we are talking to ourselves are *negative*? With everything we hear from others about ourselves, whatever news we see or hear, or no matter what's going on in our lives, no one can put us down as we ourselves can: *I'm not good enough, smart enough or pretty enough. I'm too fat, too thin, too old or not old enough. No one likes me. I'm not worthy. I hate myself.*

I believe that a head full of negative thoughts is like swimming across the English Channel, against the tide, and with lead weights. How can you reach your greatness, your true potential, if you don't have yourself in your own corner?

So, is there anything you can do about it? Yes: *watch what you say when you talk to yourself.* All you need to do is reprogram what you say to yourself, replacing negative perceptions with something positive. It may not be easy, and like anything in life, it didn't happen overnight, so don't expect it to go away overnight.

Take small steps, every
single day of your life,
and start taking
control of what you say
when you talk to
yourself.

# *Focus, Focus, Focus*

The *only* way you are going to achieve your goals is to convince yourself *you are* going to make it. Not only do you have to want it, you have to know in your head and in your heart, without a shred of doubt, that you will – not can, but will – accomplish your task.

The key word is *focus*. When you channel your energies on what you can accomplish it replaces your self-inflicted apprehension. You simply replace your negativity, your fear, your whatever, with something indisputable.

Focus, focus, focus. In everything you do and say, ask yourself these three important questions. Where are you at right now in your life? What are you truly doing to better yourself or your situation? And where on earth are you going?

If you have no goals or the self-belief that you can accomplish them, you will end up going nowhere.

Focus, focus, focus: Where are you at in your life? What are you doing to make things better? And where are you going?

# Turn Adversity to Your Advantage

There are times when negative words or situations aren't all that detrimental. Sometimes they can literally force us to 'step up to the plate'. All of us have had to cram for that test, muster up more strength during a sporting event or work smarter at the workplace. And as you well know, our results were far better than we expected.

At times, in the middle of my crusade, when the odds are against me, I go into overdrive. In the end, no matter the results, I'm more appreciative. I can be proud that I gave it my all. When I see that 'finger of defeat' pointed in my direction, I take a deep breath and from deep within my heart, I smile.

A little bit of adversity
can help to realign you,
make you humble and
make you want
it more.

## 'Big Mistake! Huge!'

Years ago a friend of mine, Tina, was in the middle of an emotionally trying divorce and had committed herself to losing some weight – against her former husband's expectations. She informed me that during their relationship, Tina's husband constantly berated her about her size. In the beginning my friend wanted to lose weight, mainly out of spite. Tina's goal was to step into their favourite restaurant, wearing a black spaghetti-strap dress, with all eyes – especially her ex's – on her. As motivation can be a valuable tool, Tina was able to rid herself of the weight quicker, when I convinced her to do it for herself and not just for revenge.

And, yes, Tina waltzed into the restaurant. And, yes, all eyes were on her. Her former husband's mouth had to be scraped up from the floor, and everyone was astounded when Tina, who once had been shy and soft-spoken, now waved her freshly manicured red fingernail at this man and uttered, 'Big mistake! Huge!'

# Deflect the Negative

None of us can escape negativity; it's only how we deal with it that truly matters.

So, how do you survive negativity? I don't mean to be crude – as I know no other way to tiptoe around this matter – but when you hear or become exposed to crap or when others go out of their way to fling mud in your direction, you've got to wipe it off and flush everything away, as soon as you can, before it contaminates your brain. Replace negativity with something positive. Immediately!

Tell yourself, 'I've been through worse before, so I can certainly do this.' 'I never did mind the *little* things.' Take a step back, collect yourself and calmly state, 'It's okay.' 'It's not that bad.' 'I'm going to be fine.' Get into the habit. Deflect the negative. As you would a pestering bug, swat it away.

*It's mind over matter —
you don't mind all the
crap 'out there' because
none of it matters!*

# Surround Yourself with a Positive Environment

Another way of deflecting negativity is to surround yourself with a positive environment. When facing the everyday sludge that life can throw at us, I think of a positive environment as a protective shield. Family, friends, loved ones, that close-knit group at work and at church, and other specialized organizations are the perfect outlet to draw inspiration, become motivated, and even gain a shoulder to lean on.

We've all heard those seemingly insignificant words 'I'm proud of you,' 'Don't give up,' 'You can do it,' but isn't it amazing the absolute power of those words coming from someone you know and trust? To me *that's* the value of a positive environment.

But a positive environment isn't about being told only what we want to hear – it can also be a hard dose of reality for us when needed.

*Draw support from those you know and trust.*

## Tough Love

*After years of living an internal hell, Oprah Winfrey's life turned for the better when she moved in with her father, a caring but 'no-nonsense' individual. Through the many interviews I've seen and read about Ms Winfrey, she credits her father's tough love for helping make her the woman she is today. While surrounding her with encouragement and praise, it is said that Ms Winfrey's father also made sure that Oprah read everything she could lay her hands on, and above all expected nothing but the best from her.*

# Create a Positive Internal Environment

Have you seen those folks that are constantly chipper? For them the glass is half full. Their enthusiasm is infectious. *They create their own positive environment from within.* Now for some, these folks might seem downright odd. But those are the folks going places!

What's your internal environment like? Do you needlessly rant and complain? Do you find yourself too defensive? Or are you optimistic? When you're feeling blue, do you wallow in your own abyss of doom and gloom, or do you go out of your way to brighten other people's day?

Again, it's up to you. It's all a matter of weeding out the bad and cultivating more productive thoughts. Every day see the brighter side of things. Continuously tell yourself how lucky you are, how good your life is right now and how things can only get better.

With a positive mind and a nurturing environment, what can you not truly accomplish? You keep a clear head and an optimistic attitude – day in and day out – and you will see a miraculous difference! This I guarantee!

With a positive mind
and a nurturing
environment, you will
live a more fulfilling,
productive life.

# A Final Word

As I close, please permit me to say that it has been an honour for me. I hope the time we spent together will enable you to live your life with a little more dignity, honour and a sense of conviction.

If you walk away with nothing else, please take with you the knowledge that nothing can dominate the hunger, the unstoppable drive, of the human spirit. *Nothing.* Not the test of time, any technology mankind can devise or any form of oppression – no matter how monumental. Nothing comes close to matching the determination from within you! The only element stopping you is you.

With all my heart I wish you Godspeed on all your journeys and God's blessings on your endeavours. I wish you my very best. Live a good life. Be happy.